Heartland Publishing, LLC

www.TicTalkBook.com

Publisher's Cataloging-in-Publication Data

Peters, Dylan, 1997-
   Tic talk: a 9-year-old boy's true story about living with tourette
syndrome / by Dylan Peters.
      p. cm.
   ISBN-13: 978-0-9981648-0-9 (pbk.)
   eISBN: 978-0-9981648-1-6 (eBook)
   1. Peters, Dylan, 1997---Mental health--Juvenile literature.
2. Tourette syndrome in children--Patients--Biography--Juvenile literature.
I. Title.
   RJ496.T68P48 2009
   618.92'830092--dc22
   [B]
                              2009019245

Printed in the United States of America

10 9 8 7 6 5 4

Previously published by Little Five Star, a division of Five Star Publications, Inc.

TiC TALK
Living with Tourette Syndrome
A 9-year-old boy's story in his own words

by
DYLAN PETERS

Illustrations; Zachary Wendland

Editor: Paul Howey

Project Manager: Sue DeFabis

Cover Design and Painting: Kris Taft Miller

Interior Design: Linda Longmire

DEDiCATiON

This book is dedicated to my loving parents who have supported me from my diagnosis and to my caring teacher, Mrs. Rita Sudhalter, for being so understanding about my TS and for giving me the idea for this story.

TIC 4 TALK

ACKNOWLEDGEMENTS

Thanks to Mrs. Rita Sudhalter and Mrs. Nancy Olson for providing me the opportunity and the resources to write this book.

A special thanks to my mom and dad for believing in me and standing beside me through everything. Thanks to Leighton and Brooke for never teasing me or telling me to stop my tics. Thanks to all of my family members for loving me unconditionally.

Thanks to Jim Eisenreich, former Major League Baseball Player, who also suffers from Tourette Syndrome, for inspiring me to reach to the stars and never look back.

FOREWORD

Tourette Syndrome has been a major part of my life since I was about six years old. I'm now well into my 40 something's and think that I've been a part of all the aspects of Tourette's. As a young boy growing up in central Minnesota, I remember thinking I was the only person in the world with this problem. I had a lot of questions about what my chances in life were going to be. Could I get a job? Would I ever have the chance to get married and maybe have kids of my own? And was I always going to be doing these things that we now call tics? Of course, the only person I ever asked these questions of was myself.

As I got older and had the chance to play Major League Baseball, I was given many opportunities to tell my story. My hope was that children and their families could get those answers to the questions I had when I was young and get them a lot sooner.

Dylan Peters is nine years old and has Tourette Syndrome. Dylan has written this book about his own personal story. As you read, you'll find that he has some of the same questions about Tourette's as do most of us with the disorder. The thing that makes this book stand out from any other that I've read is that Dylan explains everything.

He even gives definitions and spellings of words and phrases that are used when talking about Tourette's. He also makes it easy to understand for anybody that is interested. To add to this "masterpiece," Dylan has enlisted a friend to do the illustrations.

As you can see, Dylan has done what most of us (including me) would not even think of doing, especially at such a young age. He's had the questions, but instead of waiting for the answers, he went ahead and made his own. That's TREMENDOUS.

— Jim Eisenreich

Jim Eisenreich is a former Major League Baseball Player. His career covered 14 years with five different teams, including the Minnesota Twins, Kansas City Royals, Philadelphia Phillies, Los Angeles Dodgers, and the 1997 World Series Champion Florida Marlins. He is an active member of the national Tourette Syndrome Association and Founder of the Jim Eisenreich Foundation for Children with Tourette Syndrome. He strives for public awareness and is a significant participant in fundraising efforts for Tourette Syndrome.

TIC 7 TALK

Hy name is Dylan, and I am going to be in third grade in a couple of weeks. I love to play sports like soccer, football, and baseball. My favorite subjects in school are reading and math. I also enjoy playing with my older brother, Leighton, my younger sister, Brooke, and my dad.

My favorite subjects in school are reading and math.

This summer has been great. We moved into a new house, played baseball games twice a week, went to camp, and went swimming a lot! A week ago, my mom saw me making a bunch of strange body movements (mostly with my face). She asked me if these were new "tics." She asked me if I was stressed out and worried about starting school. All this talk about tics may confuse you a little bit, so I'll flash back to the beginning of preschool.

This summer has been great.

I looked like a robot with all the wires stuck to my head.

When I was about four, I started to jerk my head uncontrollably. My mom and dad didn't know why and decided to take me to a pediatrician (pe·di·a·tri·cian – a children's doctor). My pediatrician said we should go see a neurologist (nu·ra·le·jist – a doctor who specializes in the body's nervous system and how the brain works).

The neurologist did some tests and even though I was scared, I was brave. (I think my mom and dad were even more scared!) The tests didn't hurt. He did a CAT scan, which is like an x-ray of your brain, and an EEG, which measures the activity in your brain.

You should have seen my head. I looked like a robot with all the wires stuck to my head. I also got to watch a movie while they were testing to keep me entertained and still. My mom got to come with me. We were both glad when the tests were over and we could go home.

It's like your brain has a mission to annoy you.

A couple of weeks later, the test results came back. There was nothing wrong on the CAT scan or EEG. Right now there is no test to determine if you have Tourette Syndrome. Since I had these body movements and vocal sounds for awhile and they were observable by the neurologist, I was diagnosed with Tourette Syndrome (TS for short). Tourette Syndrome is a brain disorder that is characterized by different types of tics. In other words, TS causes uncontrollable body movements (like double blinking your eyes or jerking your head from side to side) or sometimes repeating words, sounds, or phrases over and over (like grunting or clearing your throat). These are called tics. The biggest bummer about having tics is that you can't make them stop no matter how hard you try, and believe me I have tried! It's like your brain has a mission to annoy you and make everyone around you notice these bizarre actions.

My parents and I decided we would share with our closest family members the fact that I had TS. That was okay, but I decided I didn't want any of my friends, their parents, or my teachers to know.

By the time I started kindergarten, I was still jerking my head around and clearing my throat a million times a day – okay, maybe not a million, but it was a lot. I almost got through the whole school year without anyone knowing about the TS, but with six weeks left in the school year, my tics had become so bad that my mom and dad took me back to the neurologist. He said he wanted me to try some medicine to help reduce my tics. He told us that there was no medication that would make the tics go away. Hearing this made my parents and me very sad.

Hearing this made my parents and me very sad.

We decided to try the medication and knew that we had to tell my teacher because the medicine might make me sick. My teacher was very understanding and said that she had not noticed my tics. "Dylan, I am very proud of you for sharing this with me," she said, "and I will keep it a secret for as long as you want it to be a secret." A week later, the medicine began making me sick, and I had to stop taking it. The tics were still awful, and I was ANGRY. I couldn't wait for summer to arrive.

The tics were still awful, and I was ANGRY.

U V W X Y Z

On first grade, I would jerk my head the way I did when I was in kindergarten. I would also double-blink my eyes, which is what I call it when I hold my eyes closed longer than most people. I managed to survive first grade without anyone commenting on my tics. I think my friends might have noticed but just never said anything, at least not yet.

I managed to survive first grade without anyone commenting on my tics.

I was really looking forward to second grade. I'd started taking a new medicine that helped slow down my tics, but they were still there. I knew eventually somebody would notice. I had the same tics, plus a few new ones like opening my mouth really wide over and over and making a gurgling sound.

I was really looking forward to second grade

I remember one of my friends, Jaylen, was swinging on the playground when he asked me why I would keep my eyes closed for so long. (I knew it – someone finally asked the big question.) I just ignored him and he forgot about it. At least I hoped he'd forgotten about it.

I became more worried that more people would notice, and they did. A couple of my other friends asked why I rolled my head around and opened my mouth so wide. I just ignored them, too. I was sad, angry, and frustrated that my secret wasn't going to be able to be kept a secret forever. I kept asking, "Why me? What did I do to deserve this crummy problem?"

Why me?

If life gives you a lemon, make lemonade.

When I shared my feelings with my mom she said, "Dylan, I am going to tell you the same thing that your grandma told me once. 'If life gives you a lemon, make lemonade'." In other words, she said, many people have things or problems that they have to deal with. The best way to deal with them is to accept what you can't change and move on. After thinking about what my mom said, I realized that things could be a lot worse.

I have a really huge  decision to make.

Now that third grade is just around the corner and summer is over, I have a really huge decision to make – to share my secret of having Tourette Syndrome or not. Since my tics were pretty bad (especially the constant eye blinking), my mom thought it might be time to tell my friends about the TS. She said I would have to figure out whether I was ready, as only I could make that decision. My mom and I talked a lot about how some kids in my class might not want to be my friend anymore, while to other kids it would not matter or change how they felt about me.

"If someone decides not to be your friend, it is probably because they do not understand the TS," mom said. I decided to trust in my friends and hoped they would understand. Besides, I was pretty sick and tired of keeping this a secret. I also knew that if I told them they wouldn't ask me all the time why I was doing these strange things.

A week before third grade started, my mom and I met with my teacher, Mrs. Sudhalter. Together, we decided how and when to tell the class about my Tourette Syndrome. Mrs. Sudhalter said she thought my mom should come and help answer any questions that I couldn't answer. She would also be there in case I felt scared or alone. Of course, when we settled on the day and time to tell the class about my TS, my tics became a lot worse. That was because I was stressed and worried about what all my friends would think, say, and do. (Just in case you haven't figured it out yet – stress and worry cause the tics to go really, really crazy).

On the first day of school, I knew I wouldn't have to tell anyone because it was a short day, and we had lots of class stuff to get done. I met two new third grade students, and I wanted to show them around the school. I hoped they would be in my class because new kids never judge anyone by first impressions. Later that day, at lunch time, I was so excited because I wanted to show the new kids the playground. I was also excited to find out they were in my class.

I had so many butterflies that it ..... felt like my stomach was a butterfly net . . . . .

The next day, my new friends Jake and Conner were waiting outside for me. Together we waited for school to start. I don't think they noticed my tics, but it was all I could think about. If they did notice, they didn't comment or ask me about it. Still, I just kept waiting for someone to say something. Near the end of the school day, I had so many butterflies that it felt like my stomach was a butterfly net. I knew tomorrow I would have to share with my class that I have Tourette Syndrome and explain my tics.

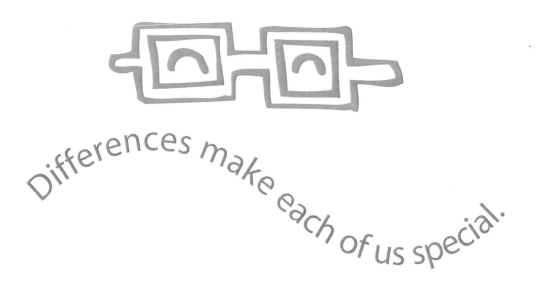

Differences make each of us special.

At promptly 9:00 A.M., I saw my mom come into the classroom. She brought a book that explained TS and what "ticing" (tick*ing – the tic movements or sounds) meant. Mrs. Sudhalter started by saying everyone is unique. She said we were going to play a "Stand Up – Sit Down" game of differences. Mrs. Sudhalter said, "Anyone who likes green beans stand up." Most of the class stayed seated. I guess there are not too many green bean lovers in the class. Then she said, "If you wear glasses stand up." A few of my friends stood up. The rest of the class remained seated. Mrs. Sudhalter explained that the game shows how everyone is different, and it is these differences that make each of us special. Mrs. Sudhalter then introduced my mom to the class and told them that I had something I wanted to share with them.

"I have Tourette Syndrome and it is called TS for short."

● was so nervous I thought I might get sick. I told myself that all of these kids were my friends and that if they were standing up to share a secret such as this, I would remain their friend no matter what. So here goes. I slowly stood up and began.

"● am unique because I have Tourette Syndrome – it's called TS for short." My class was all ears. No one had a clue what TS was, so my mom explained about how the brain decides to do things that you cannot control and these actions are called tics. I told my class about several tics I had experienced since we found out I had TS. I told them that I double blink my eyes, make a gurgling sound, and clear my throat a lot.

"I don't do these things to be silly, to get attention, or to annoy anyone. I just can't stop doing them just like you can't stop a sneeze once it starts." I told them I take medicine to slow the tics down, but that nothing can make them go away.

My mom then told the class that Tourette Syndrome is not contagious – meaning you cannot get it if you touch me or sit by me. All of my friends actually looked as though they understood. In fact, several of them made comments about themselves and how they felt unique as well.

"Just remember," I told the class, "that even though I have TS, I am the same Dylan I was yesterday, last year, and the year before that. TS doesn't change the person I am, and I hope it will not change our friendship. Thanks for listening."

I don't do these things to be silly.

Mrs. Sudhalter asked me to share the book about TS my mom had brought. My mom and I answered everyone's questions, and then she decided it was time for her to leave. My mom said to me, "Dylan, I am very proud of you and want you to know that you were very brave today." Mrs. Sudhalter said it was time to get the school day started, and I was thrilled to hear that. Everyone got out their math books and started on their problems. Later that afternoon, I realized it was just another day and nothing was different. Everyone else felt the same way, and I was very relieved.

I realized it was just another day.

TIC 41 TALK

I wasn't scared or nervous anymore about people knowing I had TS.

Over the next couple of weeks, my mom noticed that I was having very few tics. Maybe that's because I wasn't scared or nervous anymore about people knowing I had TS. My friends remained my friends, tics or no tics. I think I was worried the most about my friends making fun of me. I'd heard that other kids with TS have been made fun of, and I feel really sad for them. So, please don't make fun of anyone because it will hurt their feelings. They might have TS or something else that they can't control.

I'm taking medication now that helps calm down my tics. They still come and go, however, and some days are better than others. I'm really lucky to have a supportive and loving group of family, friends, teachers, and doctors. I will not let TS get in my way of accomplishing my goals, and you should not let anything stop you either.

TS does not mean Terrible Student. It doesn't mean Too Slow, Too Silly, Turtle Shell or Tricky Sleuth. It can mean Terrific Supporter. Remember, Tourette Syndrome is just like allergies, freckles, or wearing glasses. It doesn't change who you are. It simply makes you – YOU!

YOU!

I will not let TS get in my way of accomplishing my goals.

10 SUCCESSFUL STRATEGIES
for working with children with Tourette Syndrome

BY BRAD COHEN
Author of *Front of the Class:
How Tourette Syndrome Made Me the Teacher I Never Had*

COMMUNICATION
A crucial component to success will be your ability to communicate with the parents and the child. Success is all about building relations in the classroom. The child needs to feel comfortable around you, otherwise, he or she will struggle not only with the academics, but also the social situations.

POSITIVE ATTITUDE
For the child to keep a positive attitude, you must do the same. You will travel many emotional hills and valleys with this child, but you must always remember that the child is looking for someone to help guide them, someone to inspire them. They want to be successful, and it is up to you to provide this success.

MAKE NO EXCUSES
Help the child see the need to be accountable for his or her actions; but at the same time, be sure to let them know you are there to support them. As always, actions speak louder than words. In other words, if you are going to talk the talk, then be sure and walk the walk. Stop yourself if you begin making excuses about how you can't help this child. Just as you set out to help every child learn to read, to write, and to do math problems, the child with Tourette Syndrome (TS) needs your unwavering support just as much as the next child.

PROVIDE OPPORTUNITIES
Give this child a chance when it may seem no other chances are being offered. For example, if you see this child usually working alone, create an opportunity for the child to work with others. Create a cooperative group and sit with these youngsters and help guide them.

EDUCATE YOURSELF AND OTHERS
You need to learn as much about TS as possible. One way is to invite the local branch of the Tourette Syndrome Association to do a workshop at your school. Or, see if you can attend one of the association's local conferences. Read books or research the Internet. If you will be working with a Tourette child for the entire year, it's important that you truly understand what that child is going through. By educating yourself, you will be prepared. Then go ahead and help educate the other faculty members and the other children in the room and the school as well. The more people know and understand TS, the more likely it is that the child will experience the joy of success.

KNOW YOUR STRENGTHS AND WEAKNESSES
As a teacher, you need to know your own capabilities and restrictions. If you see you can't handle a situation, don't hesitate to ask for help from someone who may have more experience in that area. Asking for help is a sign of strength, not weakness!

SUCCESS BREEDS SUCCESS
When you see the child succeed at something, continue going back to the strategy that created

TIC TALK

that opportunity for success. Keep doing it if and until it ceases to be effective. These children especially need consistency and routine. Let them feel success. Isn't this what we want for all children?

TREAT THIS CHILD AS YOU WOULD TREAT ANY OTHER CHILD

Give the youngster repeated opportunities in which he or she can shine. Understandably, it may prove to be frustrating; but you must resist the temptation to push them into a corner because of your own frustrations in dealing with the recurring problems. If you can't continue to provide opportunities, then do the right thing and find another teacher willing to make a difference in the life of this child. All children deserve a chance. Are you willing to give that child a chance? All it takes is for one person to make a difference in the life of a child and that child's future can be forever changed.

CELEBRATE SUCCESS

Never miss a chance to celebrate the good times. Let these special children see that they, too, can be successful. Give them stickers and pats on the back, just as you would any other child. Make them feel good about themselves and what they've accomplished. It's important to let the parents share in this recognition. Call, write, or email them about their child's success, not just about the negative incidents.

LITTLE THINGS MEAN A LOT

Try these simple things in your classroom, as they can make a big difference for the child:

• Let the child sit towards the side or the back of the room, so if he or she needs to tic, it won't distract you or the other students in the room.

• Allow frequent breaks to the bathroom or to get a drink of water out in the hallway. Sometimes a quick break will allow the child to refocus and concentrate better on the lesson being taught.

• Don't overemphasize the handwriting. Instead, focus on the content within the writing. Since many children with TS have poor handwriting, it's important that the child not fail because of this. Try to use technology to help out the situation.

• Allow extra time on tests or quizzes and perhaps permit the child to take them in a separate area away from the rest of the class. By reducing the social/emotional stress factor, it will help all the students do well.

• Break up large assignments to help organize the student. Many children with TS have difficulty keeping up with large assignments that may need to be turned in over a long period of time. Help the child see the light at the end of the tunnel.

• Remember the concept of "Requiring high quality work, while reducing the quantity of work." It is okay to modify some of the work for this child. If they understand the math concept after 20 problems, then is it really necessary to have them do all 50 problems?

• Make sure the child's Individual Education Plan (IEP) is up to date. Be sure to read what allowed that child to be successful in other classrooms and what might help that child also be successful in your room.

• Graphic organizers will help the child understand what you are teaching and where you are going with that concept. Sometimes the way you learn things is not the same way others learn them. Help the child find the best learning model for them, and then continue to use that model.

ABOUT BRAD...

Brad Cohen knows firsthand of the challenges of living with Tourette Syndrome. As a child, he was punished by teachers for his outbursts over which he had no control. Now an adult, Brad believes he has overcome his disability by living life to the fullest.

Brad is a highly respected second grade teacher in a small town just outside Atlanta, Georgia. At the outset of his career, he was named the Sallie Mae First Year Teacher of the Year for the State of Georgia. It was a long way from his own elementary school days!

In addition to his responsibilities as an educator, Brad has served on the Board of Directors of the Tourette Syndrome Association of Georgia. He started an overnight summer camp for kids with TS, and now travels around the country helping to establish other such camps.

Brad appeared on Oprah on a segment titled, "Against All Odds," and was recently featured in an article in *People* magazine. His book, *Front of the Class*, is helping inspire people to overcome whatever obstacles, whatever disabilities they may be facing.

"Never ever underestimate the power of a positive attitude," says Brad. "And never forget that a positive attitude is something each one of us can have. It's a choice we can and should make."

You can learn more about Brad and his book on his website, www.frontoftheclassbook.com.

ADDITIONAL RESOURCES

Tourette Syndrome Association, Inc.
42-40 Bell Boulevard
Bayside, NY 11361-2820
718-224-2999
www.tsa-usa.org

**Neuroscience for Kids –
Tourette Syndrome**
http://faculty.washington.edu/chudler/
ts.html

Kids Health – Tourette Syndrome
Editor-in-Chief/Founder, KidsHealthChief
Executive, Nemours Center for Children's
Health MediaNemours Foundation
http://kidshealth.org/kid/health_problems/
brain/k_tourette.html

**Jim Eisenreich Foundation for
Children with Tourette Syndrome**
Post Office Box 953
Blue Springs, MO 64013
1-800-442-8624
foundation@tourette.org
www.tourettes.org

**The Joshua Child and Family
Development Center****
7611 State Line Road, Suite 142
Kansas City, MO 64114
816-763-7605
www.joshuacenter.com

**The Joshua Center hosts an amazing camp each
year for children with the primary diagnosis of
Tourette Syndrome.

**Front of the Class:
How Tourette Syndrome Made Me
the Teacher I Never Had**
By Brad Cohen
www.frontoftheclassbook.com

ABOUT THE AUTHOR
Dylan Peters is a typical all-American boy who loves to play football, soccer, and baseball. He's a good student, too. His favorite subjects in school are reading and math. Dylan lives with his parents, his older brother, Leighton, and his younger sister, Brooke, in Olathe, a small town in the gently rolling hills of eastern Kansas. He was first diagnosed with Tourette Syndrome when he was just four years old.

Dylan Peters

ABOUT THE ILLUSTRATOR
Zachary Wendland showed not only a passion but a talent for drawing when he was only two years old. That interest has only grown over the years. In addition to his art, Zachary is an accomplished competitive gymnast. Zachary and Dylan have been friends for several years.

Zachary Wendland

ABOUT THE PAINTER
Kris Taft Miller joined Walt Disney Feature Animation directly out of college. She spent seven years there in roles including graphic designer, art director, producer, writer, presenter and editor. She moved to Raleigh, NC in 2005 to be with her husband, Jeremy. She began working with Five Star Publications in 2005 designing book covers, marketing materials and book interiors. She continues to freelance for Disney and Five Star Publications as well as a variety of other clients around the world.